# SCIENCE MAGIC

## to SURPRISE AND CAPTIVATE

*Jessica Rusick*

**Super Sandcastle**

An Imprint of Abdo Publishing
abdobooks.com

# abdobooks.com

Published by Abdo Publishing, a division of ABDO, PO Box 398166, Minneapolis, Minnesota 55439. Copyright © 2020 by Abdo Consulting Group, Inc. International copyrights reserved in all countries. No part of this book may be reproduced in any form without written permission from the publisher. Super SandCastle™ is a trademark and logo of Abdo Publishing.

Printed in the United States of America, North Mankato, Minnesota
102019
012020

THIS BOOK CONTAINS
RECYCLED MATERIALS

Design: Aruna Rangarajan, Mighty Media, Inc.
Production: Mighty Media, Inc.
Editor: Rachael Thomas
Design Elements: Shutterstock Images
Cover Photographs: Mighty Media, Inc., Shutterstock Images
Interior Photographs: Andregric/iStockphoto, p. 8 (marker); iStockphoto, pp. 4 (kid), 9 (ice cubes), 12 (kid); Mighty Media, Inc., pp. 8, 9, 10, 11, 12, 13, 14, 15, 16, 17, 18, 19, 20, 21, 22, 23, 24, 25, 26, 27, 28, 30, 31; Nellie Doneva/AP Images, p.29; Shutterstock Images, pp. 4, 5, 6, 7, 8 (envelope, shampoo), 9 (comb, nail polish remover, can, pencils), 10 (kid), 12 (kid), 14 (kid), 15 (coin), 25 (kid), 26 (kid), 28 (soda with straw), 30 (group of kids)

The following manufacturers/names appearing in this book are trademarks: Diet Coke®, Paper Mate®, Styrofoam™, Up & Up™

Library of Congress Control Number: 2019943372

**Publisher's Cataloging-in-Publication Data**

Names: Rusick, Jessica, author.
Title: Science magic to surprise and captivate / by Jessica Rusick
Description: Minneapolis, Minnesota : Abdo Publishing, 2020 | Series: Super simple magic and illusions
Identifiers: ISBN 9781532191619 (lib. bdg.) | ISBN 9781532178344 (ebook)
Subjects: LCSH: Magic tricks--Juvenile literature. | Sleight of hand--Juvenile literature. | Optical illusions--Juvenile literature. | Science and magic--Juvenile literature.
Classification: DDC 793.8--dc23

Super SandCastle™ books are created by a team of professional educators, reading specialists, and content developers around five essential components—phonemic awareness, phonics, vocabulary, text comprehension, and fluency—to assist young readers as they develop reading skills and strategies and increase their general knowledge. All books are written, reviewed, and leveled for guided reading and early reading intervention programs for use in shared, guided, and independent reading and writing activities to support a balanced approach to literacy instruction.

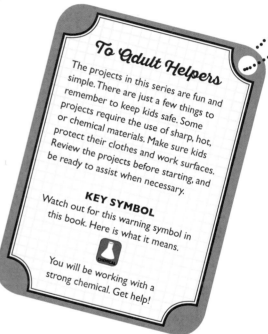

## To Adult Helpers

The projects in this series are fun and simple. There are just a few things to remember to keep kids safe. Some projects require the use of sharp, hot, or chemical materials. Make sure kids protect their clothes and work surfaces. Review the projects before starting, and be ready to assist when necessary.

### KEY SYMBOL

Watch out for this warning symbol in this book. Here is what it means.

CHEMICAL

You will be working with a strong chemical. Get help!

# Contents

# THE MAGIC OF
## Science

Have you ever seen an empty soda can refill by itself? Or Styrofoam cups melt before your eyes? These are science magic tricks!

Science tricks use every day scientific **concepts**. Many **rely** on **physics** and **chemistry** to produce seemingly impossible effects. An **audience** might never know that a trick relies on science! But many magic tricks do.

Whoa

# Tips and Techniques

Being a scientist and a magician might seem like opposites. After all, a scientist likes to explore and explain ideas. A magician likes to keep them secret! However, being a scientist and a magician are not that different. Both are curious about the natural world. They are also patient!

When following the steps to perform a science trick, read carefully. Some tricks depend on careful and **precise** movements. Others depend on chemical **reactions**. Without the right ingredients, a science trick won't work!

1 Read the steps carefully.

2 Work slowly and use exact measurements.

3 Come up with jokes and stories to **distract** your audience.

Remember, the brain is smart. Tricking it takes precision.

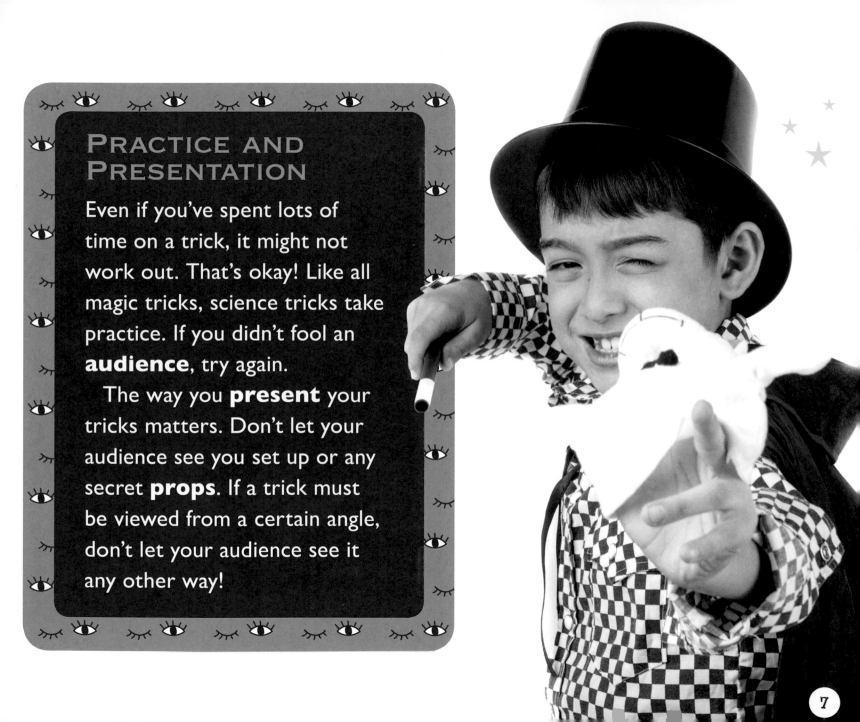

## PRACTICE AND PRESENTATION

Even if you've spent lots of time on a trick, it might not work out. That's okay! Like all magic tricks, science tricks take practice. If you didn't fool an **audience**, try again.

The way you **present** your tricks matters. Don't let your audience see you set up or any secret **props**. If a trick must be viewed from a certain angle, don't let your audience see it any other way!

# SCIENCE MAGIC
## Tool Kit

Here are some of the materials that you will need for the tricks in this book.

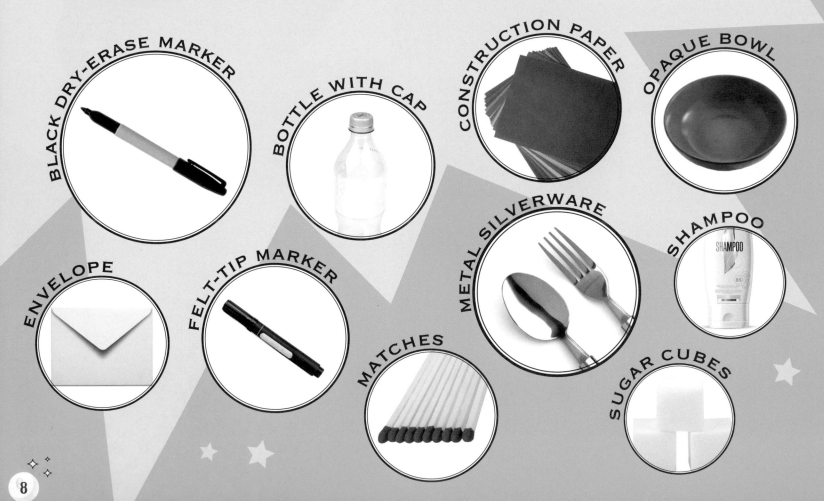

BLACK DRY-ERASE MARKER

BOTTLE WITH CAP

CONSTRUCTION PAPER

OPAQUE BOWL

ENVELOPE

FELT-TIP MARKER

METAL SILVERWARE

SHAMPOO

MATCHES

SUGAR CUBES

PAN

ICE CUBES

CLEAR PLASTIC SHEETS

PENCILS

INDEX CARDS

PLASTIC COMB

PURE ACETONE

STYROFOAM CUPS

THUMBTACKS

TOOTHPICKS

WIRE

SODA CAN

# MAGIC COMB

**Materials**
+ faucet
+ plastic comb
+ clean, dry hair

This comb bends water!

**1** Adjust the faucet until a thin stream of water comes out.

**2** Run the comb through your hair several times.

**3** Hold the comb near, but not touching, the stream of water. The water should move toward the comb!

## BEHIND THE MAGIC

When you brush your hair, electrons collect on the comb. Electrons have a **negative** charge. The negatively charged comb **repels** the negative electrons in the water. This leaves the water nearest to the comb with a positive charge. Negative charges **attract** positive charges, so the water stream bends toward the comb.

# MELTING CUPS

Make a stack of cups melt before your audience's eyes!

## Materials

+ ¼ cup pure acetone

+ large, opaque bowl

+ stack of Styrofoam cups

**1** To prepare the trick, have an adult pour ¼ cup of pure acetone into an **opaque** bowl. Don't let your **audience** see into the bowl!

**2** Tell your audience that you will make the cups melt with nothing but your hand. Place the stack of Styrofoam cups facedown in the bowl.

**3** Press the cups into the acetone. Avoid touching the liquid with your fingers.

**4** Once the cups have melted, show the contents of the bowl to your audience.

## BEHIND THE MAGIC

Styrofoam is made from a material called polystyrene. Acetone breaks the bonds holding polystyrene together. This releases the air in the material. So, the cups in this trick don't actually melt. They **dissolve**!

# ANTI-GRAVITY SILVERWARE

**Perform a seemingly impossible balance trick!**

## Materials

+ metal fork
+ metal spoon
+ match
+ drinking glass
+ water

**1** Hook the fork and spoon together so the fork's middle **tines overlap** the back of the spoon.

**2** Stick the match between the fork's middle tines. It should also touch the edge of the spoon.

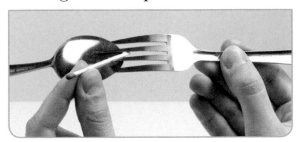

**3** Push the match almost all the way through the tines. The match head should remain on the outer edge of the curve.

**4** Fill a glass halfway with water. Place the match on the edge of the glass to balance the fork and spoon.

## PROP SWAP

You can also make a balanced structure with two forks and a quarter. Hook the forks together and put the quarter between the middle tines. Balance this on a glass just like the match structure!

# SWIMMING TOOTHPICK

Make a toothpick move without touching it!

## Materials

+ 2 toothpicks, each with a sharp end and dull end
+ shampoo
+ pan
+ water

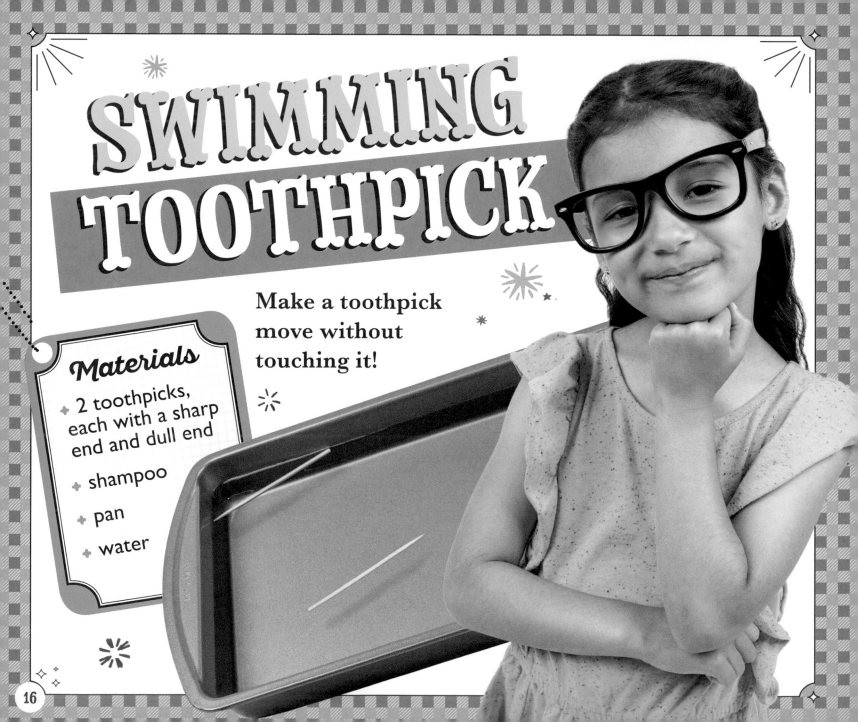

1  To prepare the trick, dip the dull end of one toothpick into a bottle of shampoo. Set the toothpick aside.

2  Fill a pan three-fourths full of water.

3  Set the toothpick without shampoo in the water.

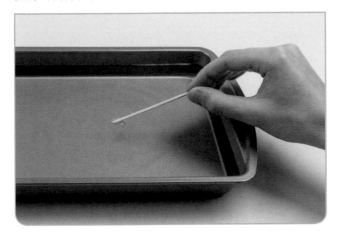

4  Ask your **audience** if they can make the toothpick swim across the water without touching it. When your audience gives up, tell them you can use magic to make a toothpick swim!

5  Set the shampoo-dipped toothpick in the water, sharp end forward.

6  Wave your hand over the toothpick. The toothpick is swimming!

## BEHIND THE MAGIC

Water molecules hold on to each other tightly. This force is called surface tension. Surface tension is what makes the toothpick float on the water's surface. Shampoo contains ingredients that break the water's surface tension. So, the shampoo-coated toothpick end breaks through the water molecules and moves.

# WIRE AND ICE

Pass a wire through an ice cube!

## Materials
+ copper wire
+ scissors
+ ice cube
+ 2 pencils
+ drinking glass

**1** Cut a piece of copper wire about 1 foot (30 cm) long.

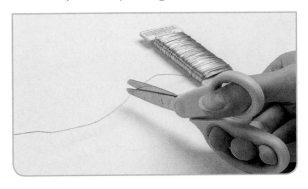

**2** Wrap each end of the wire around one of the pencils.

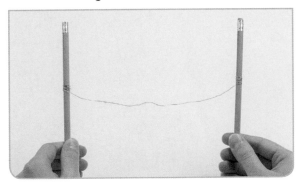

**3** Turn the glass upside down and place the ice cube on it. Set the middle of the wire on top of the ice cube.

**4** Push down on the pencils. The ice beneath the wire will start to melt.

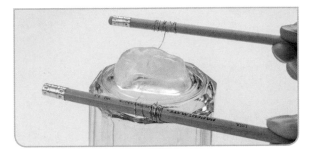

**5** Stop pushing down on the pencils. The ice will re-freeze around the wire!

## BEHIND THE MAGIC

Pressure can melt ice. So, when you push down on the wire, the ice underneath it starts to melt. Once the pressure is removed, the ice re-freezes. This process of melting and re-freezing is called regelation.

# ALL-SEEING TUBE

Read a volunteer's hidden word!

## Materials

+ dark construction paper
+ scissors
+ ruler
+ tape
+ black felt-tip marker
+ white index card
+ small brown envelope
+ large white envelope

1. To prepare the trick, cut a 10-inch (20 cm) long and 4-inch (10 cm) wide strip of construction paper.

2. Roll the paper into a tube and secure it with tape. This is your magic tube.

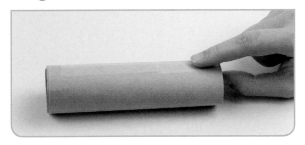

3. Have a **volunteer** write a secret three-letter word in black marker on an index card. Tell them to write the word in large letters.

4. Ask your volunteer to place the paper in the brown envelope.

5. Have your volunteer place the brown envelope in the white envelope. You should not be able to see the word.

6. Place one end of the magic tube against the white envelope. Look through the other end. You should be able to read the word!

Whoa

# MAGIC SUGAR CUBE

Transfer a number to your volunteer's hand!

## Materials

+ sugar cube

+ non-mechanical pencil

+ glass of warm water

**1** Ask a **volunteer** to pick a number between 1 and 10.

**2** Write the number on a sugar cube in pencil. Make sure to press hard.

**3** Squeeze the cube between your thumb and index finger to **transfer** the number to your thumb. Don't let your volunteer see the number!

**4** Place the sugar cube in the water and let it **dissolve.** Tell your volunteer that you can bring back the dissolved number.

**5** Guide your volunteer's hand so it is over the glass, palm down. While you do this, press your thumb against their palm.

**6** Have your volunteer wave their hand over the cup. Tell them to look at their palm. There's the number!

# ANTI-GRAVITY WATER

Make water stay in an upside-down bottle!

## Materials

+ bottle of water with cap
+ clear plastic sheet
+ pencil
+ scissors

**1** To prepare the trick, place the bottle's cap on plastic and trace around it in pencil.

**2** Cut out the circle. Keep it hidden from your **audience**.

**3** Perform the trick outside or over a large sink. Pour a little water out of the bottle to show your audience that it's full.

**4** Slowly turn the bottle over. As you do this, secretly press the plastic circle over the opening.

**5** Hold the bottle upside down. The water doesn't spill!

Wow

# EVERLASTING SODA

Make an empty soda can reseal and fill back up!

**1** To prepare the trick, use a thumbtack to make a small hole one-third of the way down the soda can. Hold the can over a sink, as some soda may spray out.

**2** Empty some of the soda through this hole into the sink. Then squeeze the top of the can so it looks slightly crushed.

**3** Color under the pull tab with a black dry-erase marker. This will make the can look open.

**4** It's time to perform your trick! Show your **audience** the "empty" can. Don't let them pick it up!

Nice!

CONTINUED ON NEXT PAGE

**5** Rub off the black marker with your thumb to secretly "reseal" the can.

**6** Hold the can in one hand. Cover the thumbtack hole with a thumb or finger.

**7** Tilt the can from side to side. The gas in the can will expand, and the can will re-inflate.

**8** With the hole still covered, open the pull tab.

**9** Pour the drink into a glass for your **audience** to try.

## ICONIC ILLUSIONIST

Jason Latimer is a magician who uses science in many of his tricks. Science helps him understand what is possible in magic! In one of his best-known tricks, Latimer makes light look like a solid object. In 2018, he co-hosted the Science Channel show *SciJinks*. Latimer used science to perform daring tricks and practical jokes.

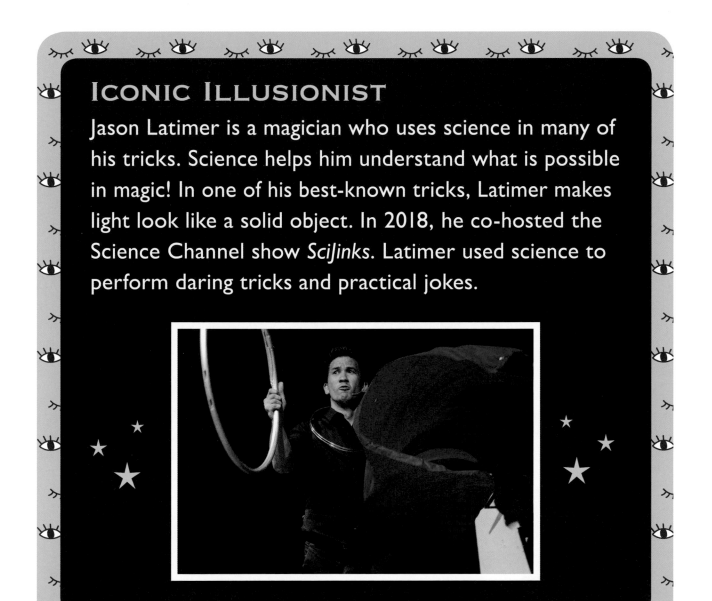

# HOST A
# MAGIC SHOW!

Magic tricks need more than **props** and practice. They also require an **audience**! When you have a few science tricks ready, put on a magic show for your friends and family. You could try setting up a stage for it. Or, keep it simple and gather your audience around a table.

Whoa

Cool

# TIPS TO BECOME A
## Master Magician

Be **confident** when **presenting** your tricks.

Use stories and other **distractions** to make your performances stand out.

Keep a trick's secret to yourself if you wish. A little mystery makes magic fun!

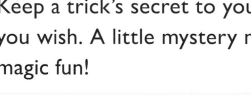

# Glossary of Magic Words

attract – to cause something to move closer.

audience – a group of people watching a performance.

chemistry – a science that focuses on substances and the changes they go through.

concept – an idea.

confident – feeling sure you can do something.

dissolve – to mix something with a liquid so that it becomes part of the liquid.

distract – to cause to turn away from one's original focus of interest.

negative – containing the electric charge carried by electrons.

opaque – not letting light through.

overlap – to make something lie partly on top of something else.

physics – the science of how energy and objects affect each other.

precise – accurate or exact. The quality or state of being accurate or exact is precision.

present – to show or talk about something to a group or the public. A performance is called a presentation.

prop – an object that is carried or used by a performer in a performance.

reaction – the chemical action of two or more substances on each other. This produces at least one additional substance.

rely – to depend on.

repel – to drive away.

tine – a sharp, pointed part of something.

transfer – to pass from one thing or place to another.

volunteer – a person who offers to do something.